Acadian
Reminiscences

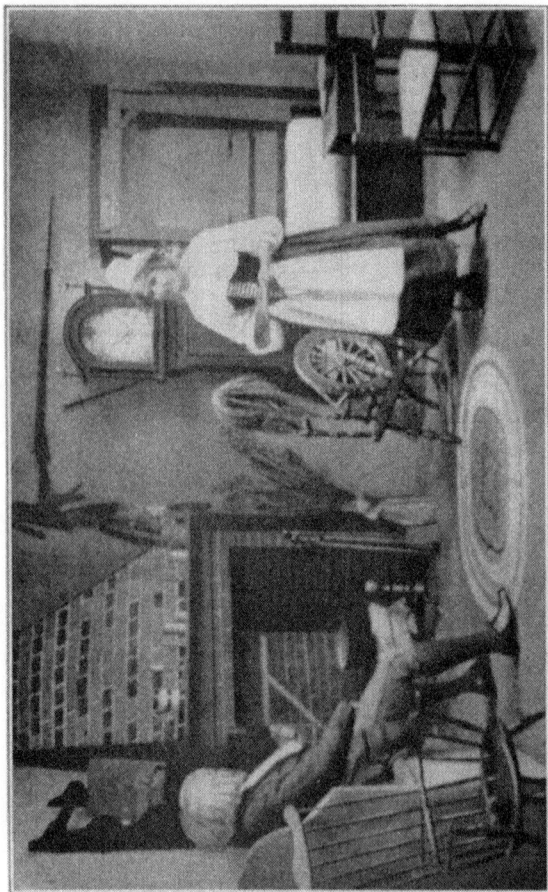

A Modern Conception of Evangeline

Posed by Rev. A. T. Kempton

Acadian
Reminiscences

With the True Story of Evangeline

by Felix Voorhies

Introduction by Andrew Thorpe

LONE STAR

LONE STAR PUBLISHING
GRETNA 2017

First Pelican edition, 1978
Second printing, 2017

ISBN: 9781565544420

Printed in the United States of America
Published by Lone Star Publishing
1000 Burmaster Street, Gretna, Louisiana 70053

Table of Contents

List of Illustrations

Introduction

The Acadian Reminiscences, is a word painting of the life of the Acadians in the Teche Country in the long ago.

The plain, simple frugal life of these people, their devotion to principle, their unbounded faith in the goodness of God, their love for each other during all their misfortunes and perilous wanderings, appeal to the heart.

The simple pathos of the grandmother's story comes to us with such consummate art, that the eye unwittingly grows moist, as the reader follows the journeyings of this little band, self-exiled and noble in their poverty, from desolated homes on the bleak Acadian coast, to their final destination in the hospitable valley of the Teche.

The entire sketch is so life-like, so real, so true to nature, that one can hardly realize that it was written by one who had not experienced the dire misfortunes that overtook these unfortunate people.

With them, we hear in their peaceful Acadian homes the first war-cry that startles the country, and shudder at the near approach of the cruel and merciless foe. We hope against hope that God or man will interfere in their behalf—till the dreaded day dawns, on which they must decide whether or not they will be

true to their God, their King, their country, lose all
and become wanderers on the face of the earth; or sacrificing these, supinely yield to Britain, and continue to
live at ease and in plenty in the homes of their youth,
and till the soil hallowed by the graves of their fore-
fathers.

When these issues were presented to them, much
as they loved their homes, and the land that gave them
birth, they cried out with one accord: "No, no a
thousand times! Sacrifice our religion, our King, our
country? No, let ruin, desolation, despair, let death
overtake us, we cannot, we will not give up those."
And so the die was cast. In the utmost haste valuables
were gathered together or thrown into wells, objects
of spoil were destroyed, and they themselves applied
the torch that soon reduced their beloved village to
ashes. In the darkness of the night, lighted only by the
lurid glare of their burning homes, they left their devoted St. Gabriel forever.

Later on we read of the separation of the colony,—
fathers and mothers from their children, husbands from
wives, maidens from their lovers; their heartless
abandonment by the English on the rocky shores of
Maryland; of kindness received by them at the hands
of Charles Smith and Henry Brent, names thus immor-
talized in Acadian history; their three years' stay in
Maryland and their final drifting through their desire
of meeting their loved and lost ones again on earth, to
the beautiful and far-famed valley of the Teche.

The writer has presented a prose pastoral, that in its unique composition, will probably bear favorable comparison with the annals of Joan of Arc, given to the world as the narrative of her secretary (told as the grandmother's narrative in these Reminiscences) which among critics has been accorded a high place in English Literature.

These Acadian Reminiscences are to be commended, and a more extended history of these ancestors is earnestly wished for from the author's pen.

ANDREW THORPE.

Chapter
One

Acadian Reminiscences

with the true
Story of Evangeline

I seems but yesterday, and yet sixty years have passed away since my boyhood. How fleeting is time, how swiftly does old age creep upon us with its infirmities. The curling smoke, dispelled by the passing wind, the water that glides with a babbling murmur in the gentle stream, leave as deep a mark of their passage as do the fleeting days of man.

I was twelve years old, and yet I can picture in my mind the noble simplicity of my father's house. The homes of our fathers were not showy, but their appearance was smiling and inviting; they had neither quaintness nor gaudiness, but

were as grand in their simplicity as the
boundless hospitality of their owners,
for no people were more generous or
hospitable than the Acadians who settled
in the magnificent and poetical wilds of the
Teche country.

My father's house stood on a sloping
hill, in the center of a large yard, whose
finely laid rows of china trees, interspersed
with clusters of towering oaks, formed de-
lightful vistas. On the declivity of the hill
the orchard displayed its wealth of orange,
of plum and peach trees. Farther on was
the garden, teeming with vegetables of all
kinds, sufficient for the need of a whole
village.

I can yet picture that yard, with its
hundreds of poultry, so full of life, running
with flapping of wings and with noisy
cacklings around my mother as she scattered the grain for them morning and
evening.

At the foot of the hill, extending to
the Vermillion bayou, were the pasture

grounds, where grazed the cattle, and where the bleating sheep followed, step by step, the stately ram with tinkling bell suspended to his neck. How clearly is that scenery pictured in my mind with its lights and shadows! Were I a painter I could even now portray with striking reality the minutest shadings and beauties of that landscape.

How strange that I should recall so vividly those things, while scenes that I have admired in my maturer years have been obliterated from my memory! Ah! the child's mind, like soft wax, is easily molded to sensations and impressions that never fade, while man's mind, blunted by the keenness of life's deceptions, can no longer receive and retain the imprints of those impressions and sensations.

If this be true, does not a kind Providence suggest to us, in this wise, the wisdom of molding the child's mind and intelligence with the fostering care of parental solicitude, that he may become

an upright man, a good citizen and a re-
proachless husband and father.

My father was an Acadian, son of an
Acadian, and proud of his ancestry. The
term Acadian was, in those days, synony-
mous with honesty, hospitality and generosity.   By his indomitable energy, my
father had acquired a handsome fortune,
and such was the simplicity of his manners,
and such his frugality, that he lived, contented and happy, on his income.

Our family consisted of my father and
mother, of three children, and of my
grandmother, a centenarian, whose clear
and lucid memory contained a wealthy
mine of historical facts that an antiquarian
or chronicler would have been proud to
possess.

In the cold winter days, the family as-
sembled in the hall, where a goodly fire
blazed on the hearth; and while the wind
whistled outside, our grandmother, an
exile from Acadia, would relate to us the
stirring scenes she had witnessed when her

people were driven from their homes by
the British, their sufferings during their
long pilgrimage overland from Maryland
to the wilds of Louisiana, the dangers that
beset them on their long journey through
endless forests, along the precipitous
banks of rivers too deep to be forded;
among hostile Indians, that followed them
stealthily, like wolves, day and night,
ever ready to pounce upon them and massacre them.

And as she spoke, we drew closer to her,
and grouped around her and stirred not,
lest we lose one of her words.

When she spoke of Acadia, her face
brightened, her eyes beamed with a strange
brilliancy, and she kept us spellbound, so
eloquent and yet so sad were her words;
and then tears trickled down her aged
cheeks and her voice trembled with
emotion. Under our father's roof she
lacked none of the comforts of life. We
knew that her children vied with each other
to please her, and we wondered why it was

that she seemed to be sad and unhappy.
We were then mere children and knew
nothing of the human heart; grim experience had not taught us its sorrowful lessons,
and we knew not that a remembrance has
often the bitterness of gall, and that tears
alone will wash away that bitterness.

She sat in her rocking chair, with hands
clasped on her knees, her body leaning
slightly forward; her hair, silvered over
by age, could be seen under the lace of her
cap; her dress was neat and tasteful, for
she always took pride in her personal appearance.

She called us "petiots" meaning "little
ones", and she took pleasure in convers-
ing with us. My father remonstrated with
her because she fondled us too much.
"Mother", he would say, "you spoil the
children"; but she heeded not his words
and fondled us the more. These details
are interesting to none but myself, and I
dwell, perhaps, too long upon them. Alas!
I am an old man, reviewing the joys and

sorrows of my boyhood, and it seems to me that I have become once more a little child when I speak of days gone by, and when I recall the memory of those I loved so well and who are no more.

I shall now attempt to repeat the story of my grandmother's misfortunes, and as she has related it to us time and again.

Chapter
Two

My Grandmother's Narrative

She Depicts Acadian Manners and Customs

"PETIOTS," she said, "my native land is situated far, far away, up north, and you would have to walk during many months to reach it; you would have to cross rivers deep and wide, go over mountains looming up thousands of feet, and beneath impending rocks, shadowing yawning valleys; you would have to travel day and night, in endless forests, among hostile Indians, seeking an opportunity to waylay and murder you.

"My native land is called Acadia. It is a cold and desolate region during winter, and snow covers the ground during several months of the year. It is rocky, and huge and rugged stones lie strewn over the surface of the ground in many places, and one must struggle hard for a livelihood there, especially with the poor and meagre tools possessed by my people. My country is not like yours, diversified by rolling and gentle hills, covered the year round with a thick carpet of green grass, and where every plant sprouts up and grows to maturity as if by magic, and where one may enrich himself easily, provided he fears God and is laborious and economical. Yet I grieve for my native land, with its rocks and snows, because I have left there a part of my heart in the graves of those I loved so well and who sleep under its sod."

And as she spoke thus, her eyes streamed with tears and emotion choked her utterance.

"I have promised to give you an insight into the manners and customs of your Acadian ancestors, and to tell you how it was that we left our country as exiles to emigrate to Louisiana. I now keep my

promise, and will relate to you all that I
know of our sad history:

"You must know, petiots, that less than
a hundred years ago Acadia was a French
Province, whose people lived contented
and happy. The king of France sent brave
officers to govern the province, and these
officers treated us with the greatest kindness; they were our arbiters and adjusted
all our differences, and so equitable were
their decisions, that they proved satisfactory to all. Is it strange, then, that being
thus situated we prospered and lived contented and happy? Little did we then
dream of what cruel fate had in store for
us.

"Our manner of living in Acadia was
peculiar, the people forming, as it were,
one single family. The province was di-
vided into districts inhabited by a certain
number of families, among which the government parceled out the land in tracts
sufficiently large for their needs. Those
families grouping together formed small

villages, or posts, under the administration
of commandants.   No one was allowed to
lead a life of idleness, or to be a worthless
member of the province.   The child
worked as soon as he was old enough to do
so, and he worked until old age unfitted him
for toil.   The men tended the flocks and
tilled the land, and while they plowed the
fields, the boys followed them step by step,
goading on the work-oxen.   The wives
and daughters attended to the household
work, and spun the wool and cotton which
they wove and manufactured into cloth
with which to clothe the family.   The old
people not over active and strong, like
your grandmother,'' she would add with
a smile, ''together with the infirm and in-
valids, braided the straw with which we
manufactured our hats; so that you see,
petiots, we had no drones, no useless
loungers in our villages, and every one
lived the better for it.

   ''The land allotted to each district was di-
vided into two unequal parts; the larger
portion was set apart as the tillage ground,

and then parceled out among the different
families; and yet the clashing of interests,
resulting from that community of rights,
never stirred up any contentions among
your Acadian ancestors.

"Although poor, they were honest and
industrious, and they lived contented with
what little they had, without envying their
neighbors, and how could it be otherwise?
If any one was unable to do his field
work because of illness, or of some other
misfortune, his neighbors flew to his assistance, and it required but a few days'
work, with their combined efforts to weed
his field and save his crop.

"Thus it was that, incited by noble and
generous feeling, the inhabitants of the
province seemed to form one single family,
and not a community composed of separate
families.

"These details, petiots, are tedious to
you, and you would rather that I should
tell you stories more amusing and captivat-
ing."

"No, grandmother, we feel more and

more interested in your narrative. Speak
to us of Acadia, your native land, which
we already love for your sake."

"Petiots", she said, " I love my Acadia,
and you will learn to love it also, when you
shall have been made acquainted with the
worth of its honest and noble inhabitants;
besides," added she, with a sad smile,
"the gloomy and sombre part of my story
remains to be told. When you shall have
listened to it, you will then understand why
it is that I feel sad and weep, when the
remembrances of the past come crowding
in my heart. But to resume: contiguous to
the village ground lay the pasture grounds,
well fenced in, and which were known as
the common. In these grounds, the
cattle of the colonists were kept, and thus
secured in that safe enclosure, our herds
increased every year. Thus you see,
petiots, we lacked none of the comforts of
life, and although not wealthy, we were
not in want, as our wishes were few and
easily satisfied.

"Plainness and simplicity of manners are the mainsprings of happiness, and he that wishes for what he may never have or acquire, must be miserable, indeed, and worthy of pity. Alas! that this simplicity of our Acadian manners should have already degenerated into extravagance and folly! Ah! the Acadians are losing, by degrees, the remembrance of the traditions and customs of the mother country; the love of gold has implanted itself in their hearts, and this will bring no happiness to them. Ere you live to be as old as I," she would say shaking her head mournfully, "you will find out that your grandmother is right in her prediction.

"In Acadia, as we prized temperance, sobriety and simplicity of manners more than riches, early marriages were highly favored. Early marriages foster the virtues which give to man the only true happiness, and from which he derives health and longevity.

"No obstacle was thrown in the way of

a loving couple who desired to marry.
The lover accepted by the maiden obtained
the ready consent of the parents, and no
one dreamed of inquiring whether the
lover was a man of means, or whether the
destined bride brought a handsome dowry,
as we are wont to do nowadays. Their
mutual choice proved satisfactory to all;
and, indeed, who better than they could
mate their hearts, when they alone were
staking their happiness on the venture?
and, besides, it is not often that marriages
founded on mutual love turn out badly.

"The bans were published in the village
church, and the old curate, after admonish-
ing them of the sacredness of the tie that
bound them forever, blessed their union,
while the holy sacrifice of mass was being
said. Petiots, it is useless for me to describe the marriage ceremony and the re-
joicings attending the nuptials, as you have
witnessed the like here, but I will speak
to you of an old Acadian custom which
prevails no more among us, one which we
no longer observe.

"As soon as the marriage of a young couple was determined, the men of the village, after having built a cozy little home for them, cleared and planted the land parceled out to them; and while they so generously extended their aid and assistance, the women were not laggards in their kindness to the bride. To her they made presents of what they deemed most necessary for the comfort and utility of her household, and all this was done and given with honest and willing hearts.

"Everything was orderly and neat in the home of the happy couple, and after the marriage ceremony in the church and the wedding feast at the home of the bride's father, the happy couple were escorted to their new home by the young men and the young maidens of the village. How genial was the joy that warmed our hearts and brightened our souls on these occasions; how noisy and light the gaiety of the young people; how unalloyed their merriment and happiness!

Chapter
Three

Rumors of War Disturb
the Peace and Quiet

of the Acadians

THUS far, petiots, I have briefly depicted to you the simple manners and customs of the Acadians. I will now relate to you what befell them, and how a cruel war sowed ruin and desolation in their homes; I will tell you how they were ruthlessly treated by the English, driven away from Acadia, and despoiled of all their worldly goods and possessions; how they were scattered to the four winds as wretched exiles, and how the very name of their country was blotted out of existence. My narrative will not be gay, petiots, but it is meet and proper that you should know these things, and that you should learn

them from the lips of the witnesses themselves.

"It was on a Sunday, I remember this as
if it were but yesterday, we were attending
mass, and when our old curate ascended
his pulpit, as he was wont to do every Sunday, he announced to us that war was
being waged between France and England.
"My children," said he in sad and solemn
tones, "you may expect to witness awful
scenes and to undergo sore trials, but God
will not forsake you if you put your trust in
his infinite mercy"; and then kneeling
down, he prayed aloud for France, and we
all responded to his fervent voice, and said
amen! from the depths of our hearts.   A
painful silence prevailed in the little church
until mass was over; it seemed as if every
one of us was attending the funeral of a
member of his family.   As we left the
church, the people grouped themselves on
all sides to discuss the sad news. There
was no dancing on the greensward in front
of the little church that day, petiots, and

we retired mournfully and quietly to our homes.

"This intelligence troubled us, and we tried, in vain, to shake off the gloom that darkened our souls. When we conversed together, the words died on our lips, and our smiles had the sadness of a sob.

"Ah! Petiots, war, with its train of evils and of woes, is always a terrible scourge, and it was but natural that we should ponder mournfully on its consequences and dread the future. England had enlisted hundreds of Indians in her armies, and we knew that the bloodthirsty savages spared no one, and inflicted the most exquisite tortures on their prisoners; they dreamed of nothing but incendiarism and massacre, and these were the troops that were to be let loose upon us. The mere thought of facing such fiends, was enough to dismay the stoutest heart and to disturb the peace and quiet of a community like ours. We knew not what to resolve, but, come what may, we were determined to die, rather

than become traitors to our King and to
our God.

"Then we argued ourselves into a different mood by thinking that this news might,
after all, be exaggerated, and that our apprehensions were unfounded. Why should
England wage war upon us? Acadia, so
poor, so desolate, so sparsely peopled, was
surely not worth the shedding of a
single drop of blood for its conquest. The
storm would pass by without even ruffling
our peace and tranquillity. We argued
thus to rid ourselves of the gloomy forebodings that troubled us, but despite our
endeavors, our fears haunted us and made
us despondent and miserable.

"The news that reached us, now and
then, were far from being encouraging.
France, whelmed in defeat, seemed to have
abandoned us, the English were gaining
ground, and our Canadian brothers were
calling for assistance. Several of our young
men resolved to join them to fight the
battles of France and to die for their
country, if God so willed it.

"Ah! Petiots, that was a sad day in the colony, and we all shed bitter tears. The brave young men that were sacrificing their lives so nobly, wept with us, but remained as firm as rocks in their resolve. We had, at last, realized the fact that the threatening ruin was frowning upon us, and that it had struck at our very hearts.

" On the day of their departure, the noble young men received the holy communion, kneeling before the altar, and they listened to the encouraging words of the old curate, while every one wept and sobbed in the little church. After having told them to serve the king faithfully and to love God above all else, he gave them his blessing, while big tears rolled down his cheeks. Alas! how could he look upon them without emotion and grief? He had christened them when they were mere babes; he had watched them grow to manhood; he knew them as I know you, and they were leaving their homes and those that they loved, never, perhaps to return.

"They departed from St. Gabriel, sad
but resolute, and as far as they could be
seen, marching off, they waved their hand-
kerchiefs as a last farewell.   It was a cruel
day to us, and from that moment, every
thing grew from bad to worse in Acadia.

Chapter
Four

Threatening Clouds Overcast the Acadian Sky

The Elders of the Colony Meet in Council to Discuss the Situation

"SIX months passed away without our receiving the least intelligence of what had become of our brave young men. This contributed, not a little, to increase our uneasiness, and to sadden our thoughts, for we felt in our hearts that they would never return. Our forebodings proved too well founded," said my grandmother, with faltering voice, "we have never ascertained their fate. We knew, however, that the war was still progressing, and that the French were losing ground every day. The English directed all their efforts against Canada, and seemed to have lost sight of Acadia in the turmoil and fury of

battle.   In spite of our anxiety and apprehensions, the peace and quiet of the colony
remained unruffled.   Alas! we had been
lulled to security by deceitful hopes, and
the storm that had swept along Canada,
was about to burst upon us with unchecked
fury.   Our day of trial had dawned, and,
doomed victims of a cruel fate, we were
about to undergo sufferings beyond human
endurance, and to experience unparalleled
outrages and cruelties.''

Our grandmother, at this point, was
overcome by her emotion and hung her
head down.   Awed into admiration,
mingled with reverence, for her noble
sentiments and for the ardent love she still
cherished for her lost country, we gazed
upon her in silence, and understood now
why it was that she always wept when she
spoke of Acadia.   Having mastered her
emotions, she brushed away her tears and
resumed her narrative as follows.

''Petiots,'' she said in a sweet sad tone,
''your grandmother always weeps when

the remembrance of her sufferings and of her wrongs comes back to her heart. She is an old woman and her tears soothe her grief. Scars of a wounded heart never heal entirely; joy and happiness alone leave no trace of their passage, as you shall learn hereafter. But why should I speak thus to you? Soon enough you shall learn more from the teachings of grim experience, than from all the sayings and maxims, how wise and judicious soever they may be.

"It was bruited at St. Gabriel that the English were landing troops in Acadia, whence came the rumor, no one could tell, and it would have been impossible to trace it to its source, and yet, uncertain as it was, it created considerable uneasiness in the community. Bad news travels fast, petiots, and it looks as if some evil genius took delight to despatch winged messengers to scatter the tidings broadcast over the land. The rumor was confirmed in a manner as tragical as it was unexpected.

"One morning, at dawn of day, a young man was lying unconscious on the green near the church. His arm was shattered, and he had bled profusely; it was with the greatest difficulty that we restored him to life. When he opened his eyes his looks were wild and terrified, and, despite his weakness, he made a desperate effort to rise and flee.

"We quieted him with friendly words, and he heaved a deep sigh of satisfaction. He had a burning fever, and his parched lips quivered as he muttered incoherent words. We removed him to the priest's house, where his wounds were dressed, and when he had recovered from the exhaustion occasioned by the loss of blood, he related to us what had happened to him, and we listened to his words with breathless suspense and anxiety.

"The English", said he, "have landed troops on the eastern coast of Acadia, and are committing the most atrocious cruelties. Their inhumanity surpasses belief.

They pillage and burn our villages, and
even lay sacrilegious hands on the sacred
vessels in our churches. They tear the
wives from their husbands, the children
from their parents, and they drive their ill-
fated victims to the seashore, and stow them
on ships which sail immediately for unknown lands. They spare only such as
become traitors to their Faith and to their
King. They raided our village at dusk
yesterday, and have perpetrated there the
same wanton outrages and cruelties. They
reduced it to ashes, and the least expostu-
lation on our part exposed us to be shot
down like outlaws. They have driven its
inhabitants to the seashore like cattle, and
when through sheer exhaustion, one of
their victims fell by the road side, I have
seen the fiends compel him with the buts
of their muskets, to rise and walk. I have
escaped, in the darkness of night, with an
arm shattered by a random shot, and I
have run exhausted by the loss of blood, I
fell where you have found me. They will

overrun Acadia, and they will not spare
you, my friends, if you show any hostility
to them.   Your town will be raided shortly,
and you cannot resist them, my friends.
Abandon your homes, and seek safety
elsewhere, while you have the time and
chance to do so.

"You may well imagine, petiots, that
our trouble was great when we heard this
terrible news.   We stood there, not knowing what to do, although time was precious,
and although it was necessary that we
should devise some plan for our safety and
protection.   In our predicament and
in so critical an emergency, our only al-
ternative was to apply to our old curate
for advice.

"He gave us words of encouragement,
and withdrew with our elders to his room.
We remained in the churchyard, grouped
together and speaking in whispers, our
souls harrowed by the most gloomy and
despairing thoughts.

"Ah! Petiots, we often speak of a mortal

hour, but the hour that passed away while these men were holding counsel in the curate's room, seemed to encompass a year's duration. Our happiness, our all, our life itself, in fact, were at stake and turned on their decision, and we awaited that decision in dreadful suspense. At last our elders, accompanied by our old curate, sallied out of that house with sorrowful countenances, but with steady step and firm resolve written on their brows."

Chapter
Five

The Acadians resolve to leave Acadia as exiles

rather than submit to English rule — Before leaving St. Gabriel, they apply the torch to the houses, and it is swept away by the flames.

THEIR countenance bespoke the gravity of the situation, far more serious, indeed, than we then realized, and as they approached us, in the deathlike silence that prevailed, we could distinctly hear the throbbings of our hearts. We were impatient to learn our fate, and yet we dreaded the disclosure. Our anxiety was of short duration, and one of our elders spoke as follows. I repeat his very words, for as they fell from his lips with the solemn sound of a funeral knell, they became engraved upon my heart. "My good friends," said he, "our hopes were illusory and the future is big with ominous

threats for us. A cruel and relentless
enemy is at our doors. The story of the
wounded man is true; the English are ap-
plying the torch to our villages, and are
spreading and scattering ruin as they advance. They spare neither old age nor
infirmity, neither women nor children, and
are tender-hearted only to renegades and
apostates. Are you ready to accept these
humiliating conditions, and to be branded
as traitors and cowards?"

"Never," we answered; "never! Rather
proscription, ruin and death."

"My friends," he added, "exile is ruin;
it is despair; it is desolation. Pause a while
and reflect, before forming your resolve."

"Not one of us flinched, and without
hesitancy, we all cried out: "Rather than
disown our mother country and become
apostates, let exile, let ruin, let death, be
our lot."

"Your answer is noble and generous,
my good friends, and your resolve is
sublime," said he ; "then let exile be our

lot. Many a one has suffered even more
than we shall suffer and for causes less
saintly than ours. Let us prepare for the
worst, for to-day, we bid adieu forever,
perhaps to Acadia, to our homes, to the
graves of those we loved so well. We leave
friendless and penniless for distant lands ;
we leave for Louisiana, where we shall be
free to honor and reverence France, and
to serve our God according to our belief.
My good friends, we barely have the time
to prepare ourselves; to-night, we must
be far from St. Gabriel.''

"These words chilled our hearts. It
seemed to us, that all this was a dream, a
frightful illusion, that clung to our hearts,
to our souls; and yet, without a tear, without a complaint, we resigned ourselves to
our fate.

"Ah! it was a cruel day to us, petiots.
We were leaving Acadia, we were aban-
doning the homes where our children
were born and raised, we were leaving as
malefactors, without one ray of hope to

lighten our dark future, and it seemed to
us that poor, desolate Acadia was dearer
to us, now that we were forced to leave
her forever.   Everything that we saw,
every object that we touched, recalled to
our hearts some sweet remembrance of
days gone by. Our whole life seemed
centered in the furniture of our desolate
homes; in the flowers that decked our
gardens; in the very trees that shaded our
yards. They whispered to us ditties of
our blithe childhood; they recalled to us
the glowing dreams of our adolescence
illumined with their fleeting illusions; they
spoke to us of the hopes and happiness of
our maturer years; they had been the mute
witnesses of our joys and of our sorrows,
and we were leaving them forever. As
we gazed upon them, we wept bitterly,
and in our despair, we felt as if the sacrifice was beyond our strength. But our
sense of duty nerved us, and the terrible
ordeal we were undergoing did not shake
our resolve, and submitting to the will of

God, we preferred exile and poverty, with their train of woes and humiliations, before dishonoring ourselves by becoming traitors and renegades.

"In the course of the day our grief increased, and the scenes that took place were heart-rending. I never recall them without shuddering.

"Our people, so meek, so peaceable, became frenzied with despair. The women and children wandered from house to house, wailing and uttering piercing cries. Every object of spoil was destroyed, and the torch was applied to the houses. The fire, fanned by a too willing breeze, spread rapidly, and in a moment's time, St. Gabriel was wrapt in a lurid sheet of devouring flames. We could hear the cracking of planks tortured by the blaze; the crash of falling roofs, while the flames shot up to an immense height with the hissing and soughing of a hurricane. Ah! Petiots, it was a fair image of pandemonium. The people seemed an army of fiends, spreading ruin and desolation in their path. The work-oxen were killed, and a few among us, with the hope of a speedy return to Acadia, threw our silver-ware into the wells. Oh, the ruin, the ruin, petiots ; it was horrible.

"We left St. Gabriel numbering about three hundred, whilst the ashes of our burning houses, carried by the wind, whirled past us like a pillar of light to guide our faltering steps through the wilderness that stretched before us.

Chapter
Six

A Night of Terror and of Misery. The Exiles are Captured by the English Soldiery

*Driven to the seashore and embarked for deportation
--They are thrown as cast-aways on the Maryland shores--The hospitality and generosity
of Charles Smith and of Henry Brent*

A darkness came, we cast a sad look toward the spot where our peaceful and happy St. Gabriel once stood. Alas, we could see nothing but the crimson sky reflecting the lurid glare of the flames that devoured our Acadian villages.

"Not a word fell from our lips as we journeyed slowly on, and as night came its darkness increased our misery, and such was our dejection, that we would have faced death without a shudder.

"At last we halted in a deep ravine shadowed by projecting rocks, and we sat down to rest our weary limbs. We built no fires and spoke only in whispers, fear-

ing that the blazing fire, that the least
sound might betray us in our place of con-
cealment; with hearts failing, oppressed
with gloomy forebodings, the events of the
day seemed to us a frightful dream.

"Oh! that it only had been a dream,
petiots! Alas! it was a sad reality, and yet
in our wretchedness, we could hardly
realize that these events had actually happened.

"Our elders had withdrawn a few paces
away from us to decide on the best course
to pursue, for, in the hurry of our departure, no plan of action had been
decided upon, our main object being to
escape the outrages and ill-treatment of a
merciless and cruel soldiery. It was decided to reach Canada the best way we
could, after which, after crossing the great
northern lakes, our journey was to be overland to the Mississippi river, on whose
waters we would float down to Louisiana,
a French colony inhabited by people of
our own race, and professing the same
religious creed as ours.

"But to carry out this plan, petiots, we had to travel thousands of miles through a country barren of civilization, through endless forests, and across lakes as wide and deep as the sea; we were to overcome obstacles without number and to encounter dangers and hardships at every step, and yet we remained firm in our resolve. It was exile with its train of woes and of misery; it was, perhaps, death for many of us, but we submitted to our fate, sacrificing our all in this world for our religion, and for the love of France.

"We knelt down to implore the aid and protection of God in the many dangers that beset us, and, trusting in His kind Providence, we lay down on the bare ground to sleep.

"As you may imagine, petiots, no one, save the little children slept that night. We were in a state of mental anguish so agonizing that the hours passed away without bringing the sweet repose of a refreshing sleep.

"When the moon rose, dispelling by degrees the darkness of night, we again pursued our journey. We made the least noise possible as we advanced cautiously, our fears and apprehensions increasing at every step. All at once our column halted; a deathlike silence prevailed, and our hearts beat tumultuously within us. Was it the beat of the drum that had startled us? No one could tell. We listened with eagerness, but the sound had died away, and the stillness of night remained undisturbed. Our anxiety became intense. Was the enemy in pursuit of us? We remained in painful suspense, not knowing what danger lurked ahead of us. The few minutes that succeeded seemed as long as a whole year. We drew close together and whispered our apprehensions to one another. We moved on slowly, our footsteps falling noiselessly on the roadway, while we strained our eyes to pierce the shadows of night to discover the cause of our fears. The sound that had startled us was no more heard, and somewhat encouraged, our uneasiness grew less.

"We had not advanced two hundred yards when we were halted by a company of English soldiers. Ah! Petiots, our doom was sealed. We were in a narrow path surrounded by the enemy, without the possibility of escape. How shall I describe what followed. The women wrung their hands and sobbed piteously in their despair. The children, terrified, uttered shrill and piercing cries, while the men, goaded to madness, vented their rage in hurried exclamations, and were determined to sell their lives as dearly as possible.

"After a while, the tumult subsided, and order was somewhat restored.

"The officer in command approached us; "Acadians," said he, "you have fled from your homes after having reduced them to ashes; you have used seditious language against England, and we find

you here, in the depth of night, congregated and conspiring against the king,
our liege lord and sovereign. You are
traitors and you should be treated as such,
but in his clemency, the king offers his
pardon to all who will swear fealty and
allegiance to him."

"Sir," answered Rene Leblanc, under
whose guidance we had left St. Gabriel,
"our king is the king of France, and we are
not traitors to the king of England whose
subjects we are not. If by the force of
arms you have conquered this country, we
are willing to recognize your supremacy,
but we are not willing to submit to English
rule, and for that reason, we have abandoned our homes to emigrate to Louisiana,
to seek there, under the protection of the
French flag, the quiet and peace and happiness we have enjoyed here."

"The officer who had listened with
folded arms to the noble words of Rene
Leblanc, replied with a scowl of hatred:
"To Louisiana you wish to go? To

Louisiana you shall go, and seek in vain,
under the French flag, that protection you
have failed to receive from it in Canada.
Soldiers," he added, with a smile that
made us shudder, "escort these worthy
patriots to the seashore, where transporta-
tion will be given them free in his majesty's
ships."

"These words sounded like a death
knell to us; we saw plainly that our doom
was sealed, and that we were undone forever, and yet, in the bitterness of our misfortune, we uttered no word of expostula-
tion, and submitted to our fate without
complaint. They treated us most brutally,
and had no regard either for age or for sex.
They drove us back through the forest to
the sea shore, where their ships were anchored, and stowing the greater number
of our party in one of their ships, they
weighed anchor, and she set sail. The
balance of our people had been embarked
on another vessel which had departed in
advance of ours.

"Is it necessary, petiots, that I should speak to you of our despair when thus torn from our relatives and friends, when we saw ourselves cooped up in the hull of that ship as malefactors? Is it necessary that I should describe the horror of our plight, our sufferings, our mental anguish during the many days that our voyage on the sea lasted?

"This can be more easily imagined than depicted. We were huddled in a space scarcely large enough to contain us. The air rarefied by our breathing became unwholesome and oppressive; we could not lie down to rest our weary limbs. With but scant food, with the water given grudgingly to us, barely enough to wet our parched lips; with no one to care for us, you can well imagine that our sufferings became unbearable. Yet, when we expostulated with our jailers, and complained bitterly of the excess of our woes, it seemed to rejoice them. They derided us, called us noble patriots, stubborn

French people and papists ; epithets that went right to our hearts, and added to our misery.

"At last our ship was anchored, and we were told that we had reached the place of our destination. Was it Louisiana? we inquired. Rude scoffs and sharp invectives were their only answer. We were disembarked with the same ruthless brutality with which we had been dragged to their ship. They landed us on a precipitous and rocky shore, and leaving us a few rations, saluted us in derision with their caps and bidding farewell to the noble patriots, as they called us. Our anguish, at that moment, can hardly be conceived. We were outcasts in a strange land ; we were friendless and penniless, with a few rations thrown to us as to dogs. The sun had now set, and we were in an agony of despair.

"Our only hope rested in the mercy of a kind Providence, and with hearts too full for utterance, we knelt down with one

accord and silently besought the Lord of
Hosts to vouchsafe to us that pity and protection which he gives to the most abject
of his creatures.   Never was a more heart-
felt prayer wafted to God's throne. When
we arose, hope, once more smiling to us,
irradiated our souls and dispelled, as if by
magic, the gloom that had settled in our
hearts.   We felt that none but noble
causes lead to martyrdom, and we looked
upon ourselves as martyrs of a saintly
cause, and with a clear conscience, we lay
down to sleep under the blue canopy of
the heavens.

"The dawn of day found us scattered in
groups, discussing the course we were to
pursue, and our hearts grew faint anew at
the thought of the unknown trials that
awaited us.

"At that moment, we spied two horsemen approaching our camp. Our hearts
fluttered with emotion. The incident,
simple as it was, proved to be of great importance to us. We felt as if Providence

had not forsaken us, and that the two
horsemen, heralds of peace and joy, were
his messengers of love in our sore trials.

"We were not mistaken, petiots. When
the cavaliers alighted, they addressed us in
English, but in words so soft and kind, that
the sound of the hated language did not
grate on our ears, and seemed as sweet as
that of our own tongue. They bowed
gracefully to us, and introduced themselves as Charles Smith and Henry Brent.
"We are informed," said they, "that you
are exiles, and that you have been cast
penniless on our shores. We have come
to greet you, and to welcome you to the
hospitality of our roofs." These kind
words sank deep in our hearts. "Good
sirs," answered Rene Leblanc, "you be-
hold a wretched people bereft of their
homes and whose only crime is their love
for France and their devotion to the
Catholic faith," and saying this, he raised
his hat, and every man of our party did
the same. "We thank you heartily for

your greeting and for your hospitality so
generously tendered. See, we number
over two hundred persons, and it would
be taxing your generosity too heavily; no
one but a king could accomplish your
noble design.''

"Sir,'' they answered, "we are citizens
of Maryland, and we own large estates.
We have everything in abundance at our
homes, and this abundance we are willing
to share with you. Accept our offer, and
the Brent and Smith families will ever be
grateful to God, who has given them the
means to minister to your wants, assuage
your afflictions and soothe your sorrows.''

"How could we decline an offer so generously made? It was impossible for us
to find words expressive of our gratitude.
Unable to utter a single word, we shook
hands with them, but our silence was far
more eloquent than any language we could
have used.

Chapter
Seven

Catholic Church, St. Martinsville, La.

Assisted by Their Generous Friends

The Acadians become prosperous, but yearn to rejoin their friends and relatives in Louisiana

THE same day, we moved to their farms, which lay near by, and I shall never forget the kind welcome we received from these two families. They vied with each other in their kind offices toward us, and ministered to our wants with so much grace and affability, that it gave additional charm and value to their already boundless hospitality.

"Petiots, let the names of Brent and of Smith remain enchased forever like precious jewels in your hearts; let their remembrance never fade from your memory, for more generous and worthier beings never breathed the pure air of heaven.

"Thus it was, petiots, that we settled in Maryland after leaving Acadia.

"Three years passed away peacefully and happily, and during the whole of that time, the Smith and Brent families remained our steadfast friends. Our party had prospered, and plenty smiled once more in our homes. We lived as happy as exiles could live away from the fatherland, ignorant of the fate of those who had been torn from us so ruthlessly. In vain we had endeavored to ascertain the lot of our friends and relatives, and what had become of them; we could learn nothing. Many parents wept for their lost children; many a disconsolate wife pined away in sorrow and hopeless grief for a lost husband; but, petiots, the saddest of all was the fate of poor Emmeline Labiche.

"Emmeline Labiche? Who was Emmeline Labiche? We had never heard her name mentioned before, and our curiosity was excited to the highest pitch.

Chapter
Eight

Evangeline

By Edwin Douglas

The True Story

of

Evangeline

"EMMELINE Labiche, petiots, was an orphan whose parents had died when she was quite a child. I had taken her to my home, and had raised her as my own daughter. How sweet-tempered, how loving she was! She had grown to womanhood with all the attractions of her sex, and, although not a beauty in the sense usually given to that word, she was looked upon as the handsomest girl of St. Gabriel. Her soft, transparent hazel eyes mirrored her pure thoughts; her dark brown hair waved in graceful undulations on her intelligent forehead, and fell in ringlets on her shoul-

ders; her bewitching smile, her slender,
symmetrical shape, all contributed to make
her a most attractive picture of maiden
loveliness.

"Emmeline, who had just completed
her sixteenth year, was on the eve of marrying a most deserving, laborious and well-
to-do young man of St. Gabriel, Louis
Arceneaux. Their mutual love dated from
their earliest years, and all agreed that
Providence willed their union as man and
wife, she the fairest young maiden, he the
most deserving youth of St. Gabriel.

"Their bans had been published in the
village church, the nuptial day was fixed,
and their long love-dream was about to be
realized, when the barbarous scattering of
our colony took place.

"Our oppressors had driven us to the
seashore, where their ships rode at anchor,
when Louis, resisting, was brutally
wounded by them. Emmeline had witnessed the whole scene. Her lover was
carried on board of one of the ships, the

anchor was weighed, and a stiff breeze soon drove the vessel out of sight. Emmeline, tearless and speechless, stood fixed to the spot, motionless as a statue, and when the white sail vanished in the distance, she uttered a wild, piercing shriek, and fell fainting to the ground.

"When she came to, she clasped me in her arms, and in an agony of grief, she sobbed piteously. "Mother, mother," she said, in broken words, "he is gone; they have killed him; what will become of me?"

"I soothed her grief with endearing words until she wept freely. Gradually its violence subsided, but the sadness of her countenance betokened the sorrow that preyed on her heart, never to be contaminated by her love for another one.

Thus she lived in our midst, always sweet tempered, but with such sadness depicted in her countenance, and with smiles so sorrowful, that we had come to look upon her as not of this earth, but

rather as our guardian angel, and this is
why we called her no longer Emmeline,
but Evangeline, or God's little angel.

"The sequel of her story is not gay,
petiots, and my poor old heart breaks,
whenever I recall the misery of her fate,"
and while our grandmother spoke thus,
her whole figure was tremulous with
emotion.

"Grandmother," we said, "we feel so
interested in Evangeline, God's little
angel; do tell us what befell her afterwards."

"Petiots, how can I refuse to comply
with your request? I will now tell you
what became of poor Emmeline," and
after remaining a while in thoughtful
revery, she resumed her narrative.

"Emmeline, petiots, had been exiled to
Maryland with me. She was, as I have
told you, my adopted child. She dwelt
with me, and she followed me in my long
pilgrimage from Maryland to Louisiana.
I shall not relate to you now the many

dangers that beset us on our journey, and
the many obstacles we had to overcome to
reach Louisiana; this would be anticipating
what remains for me to tell you.   When
we reached the Teche country, at the
Poste des Attakapas, we found there the
whole population congregated to welcome
us. As we went ashore, Emmeline walked
by my side, but seemed not to admire the
beautiful landscape that unfolded itself to
our gaze.   Alas! it was of no moment to
her whether she strolled on the poetical
banks of the Teche, or rambled in the
picturesque sites of Maryland.   She lived
in the past, and her soul was absorbed in
the mournful regret of that past. For her,
the universe had lost the prestige of its
beauties, of its freshness, of its splendors.
The radiance of her dreams was dimmed,
and she breathed in an atmosphere of darkness and of desolation.

"She walked beside me with a measured
step. All at once, she grasped my hand,
and, as if fascinated by some vision, she

stood rooted to the spot. Her very heart's
blood suffused her cheeks, and with the
silvery tones of a voice vibrating with joy:
"Mother! Mother!" she cried out, "it is
he! It is Louis!" pointing to the tall figure
of a man reclining under a large oak tree.

"That man was Louis Arceneaux.

"With the rapidity of lightning, she flew
to his side, and in an ecstacy of joy:
"Louis, Louis," said she, "I am your
Emmeline, your long lost Emmeline!
Have you forgotten me?"

"Louis turned ashy pale and hung dow
his head, without uttering a word.

"Louis," said she, painfully impress d
by her lover's silence and coldness, "why
do you turn away from me? I am still your
Emmeline, your betrothed, and I have
kept pure and unsullied my plighted faith
to you. Not a word of welcome, Louis?"
she said, as the tears started to her eyes.
"Tell me, do tell me that you love me
still, and that the joy of meeting me has
overcome you, and stifled your utterance."

The Evangeline Oak

Near the "Poste des Attakapas"

"Louis Arceneaux, with quivering lips and tremulous voice, answered: "Emmeline, speak not so kindly to me, for I am unworthy of you. I can love you no longer; I have pledged my faith to another. Tear from your heart the remembrance of the past, and forgive me," and with quick step, he walked away, and was soon lost to view in the forest.

"Poor Emmeline stood trembling like an aspen leaf. I took her hand; it was icy cold. A deathly pallor had overspread her countenance, and her eye had a vacant stare.

"Emmeline, my dear girl, come," said I, and she followed me like a child. I clasped her in my arms. "Emmeline, my dear child, be comforted; there may yet be happiness in store for you.

"Emmeline, Emmeline," she muttered in an undertone, as if to recall that name, "who is Emmeline?" Then looking in my face with fearful shining eyes that made me shudder, she said in a strange, unnatural voice: "Who are you?" and turned away from me. Her mind was unhinged; this last shock had been too much for her broken heart; she was hopelessly insane.

"How strange it is, petiots, that beings, pure and celestial like Emmeline, should be the sport of fate, and be thus exposed to the shafts of adversity. Is it true, then, that the beloved of God are always visited by sore trials? Was it that Emmeline was too ethereal a being for this world, and that God would have her in his sweet paradise? It does not belong to us, petiots, to solve this mystery and to scrutinize the decrees of Providence; we have only to bow submissive to his will.

"Emmeline never recovered her reason, and a deep melancholy settled upon her. Her beautiful countenance was fitfully lightened by a sad smile which made her all the fairer. She never recognized any one but me, and nestling in my arms like a spoiled child, she would give me the most

endearing names. As sweet and as amiable
as ever, every one pitied and loved her.

"When poor, crazed Emmeline strolled
upon the banks of the Teche, plucking
the wild flowers that strewed her pathway,
and singing in soft tones some Acadian
song, those that met her wondered why
so fair and gentle a being should have
been visited with God's wrath.

"She spoke of Acadia and of Louis in
such loving words, that no one could
listen to her without shedding tears. She
fancied herself still the girl of sixteen
years, on the eve of marrying the chosen
one of her heart, whom she loved with
such constancy and devotion, and imagin-
ing that her marriage bells tolled from the
village church tower, her countenance
would brighten, and her frame trembled
with ecstatic joy. And then, in a sudden
transition from joy to despair, her countenance would change and, trembling con-
vulsively, gasping, struggling for utterance, and pointing her finger at some

invisible object, in shrill and piercing ac-
cents, she would cry out: "Mother,
mother, he is gone; they have killed him;
what will become of me? And uttering
a wild, unnatural shriek, she would fall
senseless in my arms.

"Sinking at last under the ravages of
her mental disease, she expired in my
arms without a struggle, and with an
angelic smile on her lips.

"She now sleeps in her quiet grave,
shadowed by the tall oak tree near the
little church at the Poste des Attakapas,
and her grave has been kept green and
flower-strewn as long as your grandmother
has been able to visit it. Ah! petiots, how
sad was the fate of poor Emmeline, Evangeline, God's little angel."

And burying her face in her hands,
grandmother wept and sobbed bitterly.
Our hearts swelled also with emotion, and
sympathetic tears rolled down our cheeks.
We withdrew softly and left dear grandmother alone, to think of and weep for her
Evangeline, God's little angel.

Chapter
Nine

The Acadians leave Maryland to go to Louisiana

Their perilous and weary journey overland--Death of Rene Leblanc--They arrive safely in Louisiana and settle in the Attakapas region on the Teche and Vermillion Bayous

AS I have already told you, petiots, during three years, we had lived contented and happy in Maryland, when we received tidings that a number of Acadians, exiles like us, had settled in Louisiana, where they were prospering and retrieving their lost fortunes under the fostering care of the French government.

This news which threw us in a flutter, engrossed our minds so completely, that we spoke of nothing else. It gave rise to the most extravagant conjectures, and the hope of seeing, once more, the dear ones torn so cruelly from us, was revived in our hearts. This news was deficient, however, in one respect: it left us ignorant of the fate of those who, like us, had been exiled from St. Gabriel.

"That uncertainty cast a gloom over our hopes which marred our joy and happiness, and increased our anxiety.

"Our suspense became unbearable, and we finally discussed seriously the expediency of emigrating to Louisiana. The more timid among us represented the temerity and folly of such an undertaking, but the desire to seek our brother exiles grew keener every day, and became so deeply rooted in our minds, that we concluded to leave for Louisiana, where the banner of France waved over true French hearts.

"We announced our determination to our benefactors, the Brent and Smith families, and, undismayed by the perils that awaited us, and the obstacles we had to overcome, we prepared for our pilgrimage from Maryland to Louisiana.

"Our friends used all their eloquence to
dissuade us from our resolve, but we re-
sisted all their entreaties, although we were
deeply touched by this new proof of their
friendship. We disposed of the articles
that we could not carry along with us, and
kept our wagons and horses to transport
the women and children, and the baggage.
In all, we numbered two hundred persons,
and of these, fifty were well armed, and
ready to face any danger.

"We journeyed slowly; the wagons
moved in the centre, while twenty men in
advance, and as many in the rear marched
four abreast. Ten of the bravest and most
active of our young men took the lead a
short distance ahead of the column, and
formed our advance guard. Our forces
were distributed in this wise, petiots, for
our safety, as the road lay through mountain defiles, and in a wild and dreary
country inhabited by Indians.

"We secured, as scouts and guides, two
Indians well known to the Brent family,

and in whom, we were told, we could place
the most implicit confidence. We had
occasion, more than once, to find how for-
tunate we had been to secure their services.
We set out on our journey with sorrow.
We were parting with friends kind and
generous; friends who had relieved us in
our needs, and who had proved true as
steel, and loving as brothers. We were
parting from them, lured with hopes which
might prove illusory, and when we grasped
their hands in a last farewell, words failed
us, and our tears and sobs told them of our
gratitude for the benefits they had, so generously, showered upon us. They, too,
wept, touched to the heart by the eloquent,
though mute, expression of our gratitude.
Their last words, were words of love, glowing with a fervent wish that our cherished
hopes might be realized.

"We set out in a westerly direction, and
we had soon lost sight of the hospitable
roofs of the Brent and Smith families. We
again felt that we were, once more, poor

wandering exiles roaming through the world in search of a home.

"Our journey, petiots, was slow and tedious, for a thousand obstacles impeded our progress. We encountered deep and rapid streams that we could not cross for want of boats; we traveled through mountain defiles, where the pathway was narrow and dangerous, winding over hill and dale and over craggy steeps, where one false step might hurl us down into the yawning chasm below. We suffered from storms and pelting rains, and at night when we halted to rest our weary limbs, we had only the light canvass of our tents to shelter us from the inclemency of the weather.

"Ah! petiots, we were undergoing sore trials! But we were lulled by the hope that far, far away in Louisiana, our dreamland, we would find our kith and kin. That radiant hope illumined our pathway; it shone as a beacon light on which we kept our eyes riveted, and it steeled our hearts against sufferings and privations almost too great to be borne otherwise.

"Thus we advanced fearlessly, aye, almost cheerfully, and at night, when we
pitched our tents in some solitary spot, our
Acadian songs broke the silence and lone-
liness of the solitude, and, as the gentle
wind wafted them over the hills, the light
couplets were re-echoed back to us so
clearly and so distinctly, that it seemed the
voice of some friend repeating them in
the distance.

"As long as we journeyed in Virginia,
barring the obstacles presented by the
roads of a country diversified by hill and
dale, our progress, though slow, was satisfactory. The people were generous, and
supplied us with an abundance of provisions. But when the white population
grew sparser and sparser, and when we
reached the wild and mountainous country
which, we were told, bore the name of
Carolina, then, petiots, it required a stout
heart and firm resolve, indeed, not to
abandon the attempt to reach Louisiana

by the overland route we were following.

"During days and weeks, we had to march slowly and tediously through endless forests, cutting our way across undergrowth so thick, as to be almost impervious to light; brushwood where a cruel enemy might lay concealed in ambush to murder us, for we were now in the very heart of the Indian country, and the savages followed us, stealthily, day and night. We could see them with their tattooed faces and hideous headgear of feathers, frightful in appearance, lurking around in the forest, and watching our movements. We were always on the alert, expecting an attack at any moment, for we could distinctly hear their whoops and fierce yells.

"Ah! Petiots, it was then that our mental and bodily anguish became extreme, and that the stoutest heart grew faint under the pressure of such accumulated woes. Our nights were sleepless, and, careworn and on the verge of starvation, we moved

steadily onward, the very picture of dejection and of despair. Thus we toiled on
day after day, and night after night, during
two long weary months on our seemingly
endless journey, until, disspirited and dis-
heartened, our courage failed us.

"It was a dark hour, full of alarming
forebodings, and we witnessed the depres-
sion of our brother exiles with sorrow and
apprehension.

"But a kind Providence watched over
us. God tempereth the wind to the shorn
lamb. The hope of finding our lost
kindred stimulated our drooping spirits.
We had been told that Louisiana was a
land of enchantment, where a perpetual
spring reigned. A land where the soil
was extremely fertile; where the climate
was so genial and temperate, and the sky
so serene and azure, as to justly deserve
the name of Eden of America. It smiled
to us in the distance like the promised
land, and toward that land we bent our
weary steps, longing for the day when we

would tread its soil, and breathe once more the pure air in which floated the banner of France.

"At last we reached the Tennessee river, where it curves gracefully around the base of a mountain looming up hundreds of feet. Its banks were rocky and precipitous, falling straight down at least fifty feet, and we could see, in the chasm below, its waters that flowed majestically on in their course toward the grand old Meschacebe. It was out of the question to cross the river there, and we followed the roadway on its banks around the mountain, advancing cautiously to avoid the danger that threatened us at every step.

"That night, we slept in a large natural cave on the very brink of the precipice by the river. At dawn of day we resumed our march, and as we advanced, the country became more and more level, and after four days of toil and fatigue, we halted and camped on a hill by the riverside, where a small creek runs into the

river. We met there a party of Canadian
hunters and trappers who gave us a friendly
welcome, and replenished our store of
provisions with game and venison. They
informed us that the easiest and least
wearisome way to reach Louisiana was to
float down the Tennessee and Meschacebe
rivers. The plan suggested by them was
adopted, and the men of our party, aided
by our Canadian friends, felled trees to
build a suitable boat.

"There, petiots, a great misfortune befell us. We experienced a great loss in
the death of Rene Leblanc, who had been
our leader and adviser in the hours of our
sore trials. Old age had shattered his con-
stitution, and unequal to the fatigues of
our long pilgrimage, he pined away, and
sank into his grave without a word of complaint. He died the death of a hero and
of a Christian, consoling us as we wept
beside him, and cheering us in our
troubles. His death afflicted us sorely,
and the night during which he lay exposed,

preparatory to his burial, the silence was unbroken, in our camp, save by our whispered words, as if we feared to disturb the slumbers of the great and good man that slept the eternal sleep. We buried him at the foot of the hill, in a grove of walnut trees. We carved his name with a cross over it on the bark of the tree sheltering his grave, and after having said the prayers for the dead, we closed his grave, wet with the tears of those he had loved so well.

"My narrative has not been gay, petiots, but the gloom that darkened it will now be dispelled by the radiant sunshine of joy and of happiness.

"Our boat was unwieldy, but it served our purpose well. We stored in it our baggage and supplies; we sold our horses and wagons to our Canadian friends, and taking leave of our Indian guides, we cut loose the moorings of the boat. We floated down stream, our young men rowing, and singing Acadian songs.

"Nothing of importance happened to

us after our embarkment, petiots. During
the day, we traveled, and at night, we
moored our boat safely, and encamped on
the banks of the river. At last we launched
on the turbulent waters of the Mississippi
and floated down that noble stream as far as
bayou Plaquemines, in Louisiana, where
we landed. Once more we were treading
French soil, and we were freed from
English dominion.

"As the tidings of our arrival spread
abroad, a great number of Acadian exiles
flocked to our camp to greet and welcome
us. Ah! petiots, how can I describe our
joy and rapture, when we recognized
countenances familiar to us. Grasping
their hands, with hearts too full for utterance, we wept like children. Many a sor-
rowing heart revived to love and happiness on that day. Many a wife pressed to
her bosom a long lost husband. Many a
fond parent clasped in rapturous embrace
a loving child. Ah! such a moment re-
paid us a thousandfold for all our suffer-

Interior, Catholic, Church, St. Martinsville La.

ings and privations, and we spent the day
in rejoicing, conviviality and merriment.

"The sequel of my story will be quickly
told, petiots. Shortly afterwards, we left
for the Teche region, where lands had
been granted to us by the government.
We wended our way, to our destined
homes, through dismal swamps, through
bayous without number and across lakes
until we reached Portage Sauvage, at
Fausse Pointe. The next day, we were at
the Poste des Attakapas, a small hamlet
having two or three houses, one store and
a small wooden church, situated on bayou
Teche which we crossed in a boat.

"There, the several Acadians separated
to settle on the lands granted to them.

"You must not imagine, petiots, that
the Teche region was, at that time, dotted
all over like nowadays with thriving farms,
elegant houses and handsome villages. No,
petiots, it required the nerve and persever-
ance of your Acadian fathers to settle
there. Although beautiful and picturesque,

it was a wild region inhabited, mostly, by
Indians and by a few white men, trappers
and hunters by occupation.   Its immense
prairies, covered with weeds as tall as
you, were the commons where herds of
cattle and of deer roamed unmolested,
save by the hunter and the panther. Such
was the region your ancestors settled, and
which, by their energy, they have trans-
formed into a garden teeming with wealth.

"The Acadians enriched themselves in
a country where no one will starve if he
is industrious, and where one may easily
become rich if he fears God, and if he is
economical and orderly in his affairs.

"Petiots, I have kept my promise, and
my tale is told. Your Acadian fathers
were martyrs in a noble cause, and you
should always be proud to be the sons of
martyrs and of men of principle."

"Grandmother," we said, as we kissed
her fondly, "your words have fallen in
willing and loving hearts, and they will
bear fruit. We are proud now of being

called Acadians, for there never was any
people more noble, more devoted to duty
and more patriotic than the Acadians who
became exiles, and who braved death
itself, rather than renounce their faith,
their king and their country."

[FINIS]

¶ Acknowledgement is made of the kindness of Rev. A. T. Kempton, Lecturer on Evangeline; Rev. George W. Brooks, an authority on Acadian history, and The Soule Art Publishing Company, in loaning us photographs for illustrating this book.

www.ingramcontent.com/pod-product-compliance
Lightning Source LLC
Chambersburg PA
CBHW030023290326
41934CB00005B/459